(re)love

(re)love

Michaela Atencio

RESOURCE *Publications* · Eugene, Oregon

(RE)LOVE

Resource Publications
An Imprint of Wipf and Stock Publishers
199 W. 8th Ave., Suite 3
Eugene, OR 97401

www.wipfandstock.com

PAPERBACK ISBN: 978-1-6667-4884-0
HARDCOVER ISBN: 978-1-6667-4885-7
EBOOK ISBN: 978-1-6667-4886-4

08/01/22

to mitchell, my one.
your love teaches me.

Contents

preface.

this collection of poems spans multiple years of my life. these pieces were not written in order and do not have to be read as such. the book does follow a flow when read in order, but just as a garden contains multiple interconnected paths and winding walkways, this collection, too, is happy to be viewed from any angle and to be sat with over time.

this work was written by a queer, disabled Christian and while I do reference those particulars of my identity in this collection, you do not have to identify with any of these aspects of my life to read and glean from the words written here. I encourage you to wander this book slowly, with intent to listen, with prayer if you wish, and with an open heart. time is a powerful tool and not all plants bloom in every season, so it may take some time for the growth to become visible. please enjoy the fruit of these seeds that I have planted in the past few years of my life, and may your heart receive and benefit from the joy that the weeds were unable to choke out.

you are cherished. you are loved. you are seen. your heart is beautiful.

—m.

(re)love.

mind the step.

tumbling, turning
cascading, collapsing

hold.

know this moment.
shall you receive it again?

eyes up.

dropping, descending
falling, befriending

be at peace.

if given your life once more,
how would you love yourself differently?

mind the step.

groundwork.

dry, hardened dirt.
nothing left to do
but pick up the shovel
and make a first attempt.

this armor is tough
burnt brittle over the years
try to understand, if you must,
to break this topsoil, but truly,

this heart is weary.
let the godforsaken clay crack
and the rigid earth
give way to softer ground.

perhaps it is parched
in need of living water
that sets the soil free
and leads to growing greenery.

or maybe it is gloomy
lacking the light of
a home star, hopefully this
seasonal depression won't last

and someday, I shall be soft and fertile again.

important questions.

when was the irony
of self-love ever recognized
by this soul?

who would care
in between the breaths
as these bones shook?

what imaginings could save
the innocence
in every heartbeat?

how did each sliver
of mistrust plant itself
into this mind?

and why?

why did no one listen to me?

seattle speculations.

what does hope smell like?
I used to know it dearly
a hint of cinnamon
and good vibes

what does anything mean?

how might terror dance?
a waltz of wide eyes
and shallow breaths
and blinding, screeching silence

why should we matter?

who would shame befriend
on lonely nights?
perhaps one who is well acquainted
with both hope and terror

how will we survive this?

what might doubt grow into?
a crocus of wonderings
and wanderings
exposed to light and rain

let us sow it and see.

this is no ordinary ground.

it is a garden
of souls, all mine
each moment another self

weep today
as they have been planted
for their death.

but look
for the first sprouts
they will be up soon.

interim.

suspended
by cords, like a puppet

the past below
gravity waiting for the inevitable
downward spiral
the future above
in the near heavens
strings being pulled by who knows what

this moment suddenly expands
and you are frozen in time
breathless
enchanted
unable to stop the
floating sensation
knowing that eternity lies exactly here

but just like that
the moment has passed
longing for another chance
to feel present
you return to your body
pulled both ways simultaneously

you, my friend
deserve to be free.

dysphoric.

this cannot be.

consider me
a vain attempt
toward the acceptable
bounds of humanity

this cannot be.

I've tried to flee
every muscle tensed
it's highly disagreeable
to inhabit this body

this cannot be.

imagine me
a claim against
genesis one, simply a handful
of marsh or swamp, you'll see

this cannot be.

somehow you say this, too, is very good.

living with depression is like floating on a life raft every day.

I inhabit my existence
in the middle of the lake
I am always, *always*
close to drowning

the shores sit, scoffing, at the edges of my sight
too far away from my raft's reach
there lingers an everlasting ache in my limbs
from constantly treading water

there is no change or novelty in this void space
nothing to do but *just stay alive*
so every revolution of the sun and moon in their skies
I try, but something needs to change

I inhabit my existence
in the middle of the lake
I am always, *always*
scarcely surviving.

this pain is seen.

arizona introspections.

tonight
I write with
tear-stained face

I am lost for sleep
yet sleeplessness
hunts me
the early hour
leers

today was
supposed to be
a momentous day
I lean into
sorrow

it is a
terrible, gentle friend
on days such as these.

untitled.

I want to
punch things
peel my
rotted, molting
flesh off
this body (that I uncomfortably live in).

I want to
hurt me
take my
tears and
fold them
into origami (that floats away on the air).

I want to
fix this
aching, bitter
heart by
turning it
to stone (that cares no more for answers).

I don't feel
like I
have other
options anymore.
please help.
the end (I say with a question mark).

wander again.

as I wander
from wasteland
to wasteland
inside
I realize
my eyes
are dim
and my heart
has been closed
so I shall retry.

relearning is welcomed by this tender earth.

roots.

beneath the mulch
where the worms wander

in the dim space I hear
the moist earth's mantra

"welcome home,
here you're invited to grow in grace"

despite best intentions
I detect myself taking hold

of this unfamiliar soil
the worms whisper to me

"greetings, little seed,
reach your heart toward the heavens

but first, set some roots down."

speak.

dear heart,

you have lived
silently somber
for so long

under so many
lacerations and fractures
do you hurt?

I want you to find
your strangled voice
temper your fear

and speak, finally, your gospel.

control.

I wrestle with infinities
the ceiling fan hangs
silently above my head

an ambulance siren
drifts
through the air

I lay in the dark
and fruit flies dance
outside the bedroom door.

I grapple around
for an emotion,
a synonym for the word "thought"

I cannot imagine what it is like
to not be afraid
I wait in the anxiety

for dinner, for unconsciousness
for neat theologies
to present themselves once more

yet somehow I become aware
of the concept
that I control none of this

small as a fruit fly
yet unconsciously
I am an infinity

dinnertime, no time defines me
I am a synonym for the word "thought"
and one day, maybe

I will walk into light, unafraid.

softness, part 1: ceramic heart.

fragility of reception
divinity seeps through each corner
of this delicate temple

I am a sensitive being
and I am a giving hand
so it is no surprise

I spend much of my time collecting
the shattered pieces of this ceramic heart
off the floor every night.

softness, part 2: the gift.

please forgive me
dear heart
sometimes I just forget

that being soft
is our gift
to hold and to share

we are warrior-spirit
forged of flowers
and kind poetry.

burnt.

I met the redwoods this week
lovely friends they were

I learned that the forest fires
hollow them out
yet do not always fell them
allowing a space
for those in need to shelter there
throughout the storms

I met the redwoods in need
seeking shelter and hope

I found that the flames
that left me hollow
that left permanent burns
did not topple me
now the space in me
I can someday offer
as a safe haven
for those in need

thank you, dear giants
for a lesson well needed
a hope sought for
and a hell of a perspective.

friendship.

a family not of blood
waits beyond the chasm

a chariot, thoughtless,
you board in order to
meet your next of kin

hold tight
the choosing nears

multitudes passing
you call out to whom?
friends, meet me here

call yourself fortunate
to connect with these companions

it is a blessing beyond words these days.

whirlwind.

screams echo from my own distant thoughts
and I'm taken up away from my now
years ago, the hurricane sets me down
I'm 15.

and there is a whirlwind residing behind me
waiting for the slip of a finger
just a single academic error
to remind me that I am my grade
to claim that I would vanish into thin air
without this my name, reputation.
always in contention with my true self
I guard it as if I were a canine
and it was the newspaper at the front door
I open the front door
and worship what they think of me.

then the storm rushes in
its roar drowning out the mind
that could easily move on
from an unpleasant moment
I snap back to the present moment

it's 10:50 pm and I've just begun my last semester of college.

and the whirlwind looms closer these days
hoping to strip some shingles of identity
or crossbeams of courage from me
this tempest tries to tear, trick, twist

and turn truth to falsehoods.
it shouts that I am unworthy of peace
maintains that I am only as good as what I produce
including the words captured in this ink
and continually forebodes that forever
will feel something like this crashing ocean over my head.

but this house is not made of mere dust
king's breath resides here, love confides in colors
and I am more in his eyes than a mockingbird
the wings I bear crafted of scarlet
and third day tomb visits
somehow I know I matter.

and in this moment
I perceive a different rush of wind
pulling me back
I am 3.

my name is beloved
known by history's designer
already, I'm walking hand in hand with my brother
and though this big heart and open eyes
understand not what they will encounter
they dive into life with everything inside her.

she is not me, although I am partly she
and so I will make a living room in this gap
between time and eternity's collisions called the present.
and though the whirlwind cannot be silenced by me
it trembles in fear knowing who is in me
a new storm is coming
and I will stand unhindered by this downpour
after all, the harvest season is near

and the four winds meeting smell of a kingdom much like home.

abandoned poetry.

graveyard strolls at dusk
two years lost to this heart's rending

a corpse of heaven, time past
poetry's face, I hardly recall

gone are the days of infinite light
the truth now a blunt knife

oh, I remember the floral notes
of each verse in that season

now resting among the faint stars
dormant lies my tongue of dreams

my heartflow was at its finest
when this heart was most broken

this past harvest evening
words have simply failed.

but, God, I missed poetic breathing.

sun.

there is something to be said for daylight.

it beckons,
knows,
hopes,
discerns,
it tells the truth.

I have put down roots, now I reach my arms heavenward.

it calls,
trusts,
sings,
understands,
it recognizes me.

today, I shall receive this food for my soul.

for such a time as then.

let us recall the anniversaries in order
the silhouette of memories, overgrown and speckled
each time you thought you couldn't survive
somehow you lived, or at least the pieces of you did
    it almost feels as if you were created to suffer.

I hold in tension the affliction and affection
of that season, shadows of sorrow and warmth
each time you thought you couldn't breathe
somehow you lived, or at least your body did
    consider the ravens, they do not sow or reap.

and the quietude, your friend in unlit time
illuminating injuries and your gentleness of spirit
each time you thought you couldn't thrive
somehow you lived, even your mind did
    chasing the scent of joy hurts more than they tell you.

still, the fragments of the future whisper their secrets
the wonder of your worth and each echo of hope
each time you thought you couldn't continue
somehow you lived, some way your soul knew
    the harvest was nearer than your heartbeat.

tetelestai.

I know you
have said
I am very good
your crowning creation

so why do I still
feel incomplete?

is there a joy
further
I have yet to experience?
teach me to understand

how you have made me
so wonder-full

and you say that it is finished.

queer self.

oh, darling.

you deserve all the sun's warmth,
as one without pause or shadow.

you could drink the ocean dry
to the depths of your melancholy soul.

you must need the mountains
to bow toward your adventurous step.

you are a delight to the water lilies,
clothed in your wisdom and dreams.

oh, darling.

you are just the person you are meant to be.

pause.

the punctuation of music
lies in the pauses
stretching
swaying
the symphony's greatest asset
is time

and so it is with me.
patience is my armor
and the pauses
my motif.

(re)try.

let's be friends.

wild wondering
horrific heartflow

wait.

didn't you already
live that moment once?

dive deep.

heavy history
cautious catastrophes

I trust you.

if you are looking backwards,
why not choose compassion?

let's be friends.

healing, part 1: getting better.

there is no terror
quite like knowing
that a depressive episode
is ascending inside

the unrelenting roll
of the wave, windswept
tell me, unseen siren
how might I escape?

there is no blow like
getting better
and knowing that someday
the tide will return

arrive and recoil, day after day, healing persists.

healing, part 2: feeling worse.

this line graph
of my healing
displays a multitude
of both peaks and valleys

and though these days it trends
in the upward direction
the blessings linger in the air
courageous claims and coping skills

I must be quick to employ
my self-compassion
as needed, because joy
isn't guaranteed constantly

it is enough to let each day be itself.

I am afraid of silent prayer.

no sense can perceive
the silence that threatens me

the lack of voice
of beauty
of song
of melody
of anything

that is what I fear
not that I would hear
a noise from God to frighten me
but that I would hear nothing
from God
at all.

scratching open my soul.

consider this:
would you like to know
the ways my brain
conspires for me to die, daily?

for some reason, they say that we care more
for the broken moments than the holy ones.

perhaps we could learn:
my body believes more and more
that I will live and prosper
and that my gifts are meant to be shared.

I wander within the mystery that is my hope
the spirit-breath in me constantly flowing

imagine with me:
can you fathom
how many times my being cries out
that it does not belong here?

why have we decided that scratching open my soul
means telling you the most painful parts of me?

try to conceive:
my heart holds fast to
what I was taught all those years ago
I am loved beyond measure

might we try relearning our vulnerability
where the splintered and the sacred rest together?

we just might find heaven there.

river rest.

welcome
to the restart
the peaceful river
we all long to share and know

welcome
to the new abode
for your soul
it is kind and full of hope

welcome
to the restart
the peaceful river
drink deep, dear heart, that you may grow.

ever the optimist.

I live on the edges of the paint splatters
just around the canvas
     I am no organized religion

I seek truth in the book bindings of the universe
holding everything in perfect tension
     I am haunted by each beauty

oh, to be fully present, like a dancer
leap follows spin follows toe touch
     there is no neat packaging here

I find myself drifting in and out of time
fresh scents of the future beckoning enviously
     I forget to allow beginnings and endings

that which I desire myself to be
is nowhere close to who I am
     I must hold these longings loosely

even as anxiety fails to keep its grip on me
I rediscover what it is to be myself
     dreamer. thinker. poet. singer.

loved.

season.

hello, it's nice to finally meet you
I've known you were somewhere inside
for so long, correct me if I'm wrong
but something's new about this heartflow.

love, I can't wait to see you
embrace the total freedom
of this new season, harvest nearing
there is so much to celebrate.

dear heart, can I entreat you
to bring me on a tour
of our refurnished home, the shattered glass
now forming the windows into our soul.

oh, self, it's good to be you
I'm thankful for every revision
we went through, this one brand new
the echoes of heaven reverberate.

oh, how good it is to be free.

unknown.

standing on a precipice
unknown is all that I can see in the distance

I'll be moving forward.

and there's nothing that I'd rather have than side vision
meaning having beside-me-vision
because when I see Love is beside me
her vision is clear enough
and I can listen to her direction
it's perfection
to know my imperfections
will become redirections
and the outcomes are credited to her authorship.

she is the writer
of the flawless circumstance
and the rewriter when I'm thoughtless
first one chance
and a second when I stumble
she beckons then my humbled self
to her side again
I set my sights again
on the precipice

I don't need emphasis
on the genesis
of my perilous exodus

I'll heed only the recklessness
my God showed me
he owed nothing
yet let his blood
flow for Love
so for Love

I'll step out into the unknown.

broken.

shooting, stabbing, aching, burning
please check all that apply
check, check, check, check.

this form that I inhabit, somehow had it,
the luck to inherit the chronic cycles
of pain, is this now my name?
the spasm intensifies again.

sleepless nights, to morning half-sights
I need to find a better posture
for my rest, I feel like a guest
in my own fucking body.

this point is true, I cannot earn you
the moments of ease or lightness
in grace, please keep me in pace
with your sacred sort of walk.

this my body broken, consider it a token
this living death cannot be the end
to meaning, resuscitation intervening
there must be something to hope in.

step, step, step, step.
the Son of Man heads toward Golgotha
shooting, stabbing, aching, burning.

rain.

drink deep
pause doubt
hold hope
dark prowls

let peace
crash down
all fear
wash out

one love
called loud
drink deep
blue vows

this is living water.

belonging.

I am
not
unknown

as I drift
across
the meadow

I am
not
distant

for I walk
into
open arms

I am
not alone
any longer

for
the holy ghost
has made me hers.

when kind things hurt.

when kind things hurt
and sky falls to touch
the face of those who have wept

when death abounds
and peace flees in terror
from the land of those lied to about freedom

when purpose stalls
and money falls from hands
amidst economy designed for the few

when kind things hurt
and sky hangs heavy
little one, know this and only this:

you are wanted just for you.

dinnertime.

the cosmic mother is my friend.

she welcomes me in from an afternoon
of play in her harvest fields

dusts off my grubby face
and kisses me loudly all over

places a warm cup of soup
in front of me

"eat up, love.
you must be hungry!"

I am home here.

a new perspective on hope.

hope, that treacherous travel
stumbling through my mind

an idealist eyesore I cannot
apologize enough for

why should you tolerate my daydream?
it's not integrous to my brand

perhaps an unrealistic utopia I seek
nostalgia surely has its faults here

I find myself addicted anyway.

a letter.

dear heart
you are missed
by the waves
and the midnight whispers

little one
the lilies' faces
light up to see you
walk near their home

it's been a while
you may have more on your shoulders
than you used to
more lines around your eyes

but you
are still
holy love incarnate
don't you forget

that you are here
welcomed
by this moment
and every other

please, friend
let the north winds tell you your name
the scent of fresh rosemary
awaken your tired mind

you do belong here, after all
among the life
the noise
the color

and you are wished for
by the fireflies.

living with PTSD is like climbing a mountain every day.

the summit before me
aspiring to touch the cumuli above
I begin my ascent with my supplies,
my backbone, and a prayer

it would be much too easy
to montage these moments
but the labor of this life is a lingering endeavor
a slope demanding

I hope to one day call this my discipline
my rule of life, if you will
before I make each step
assessing the veracity of the stones ahead

there is no expeditious path
to the peak, my friends
the landscape sights must be earned
in due time and toil

but I have rehearsed this trail
many times in recent history
preparing every breath
enacting muscle memory once more

and if this tired body
holds up for me today
I shall once again revel
in the glory of the peak

the heaven of wholeness
a little nearer than the day before.

pipe dreams.

dear heart,

what else is there to say?
progress is slow here

your heartbroken, headstrong
hope for a better world

may or may not succeed.
adjust your desires accordingly.

your captivating, cautious
ascent toward self-love

may or may not be worth it.
it's up to you to decide.

what else is there to say?
yet, slow progress is here.

heavens.

when I catch the glimpses
of love creeping through
the cracks of carnal chaos
I want to trust in the goodness of the *imago dei*

but

when I see daily
the fucking maelstrom
we've worked our world into
I reconsider a doctrine of total depravity

heavens.

yet I believe deep down
that someday empire will bow
to holy spirit's redeeming creativity
her breath in us reviving embodied beauty

and

when I remember that
it doesn't have to be this way
liberation's whirlwind rends the curtain
from sin, death, and decay arise incarnate glory

heavens.

reversal.

I am time
yet today
I am sprinting backwards

flying through the memories of the seasons
I pause at the picturesque peak of the mountain
the murmured reminiscence of the footsteps
and the arduous journey to arrive right here

I clutch at the branches of the redwood trees
passing me by at lightning strike speeds
the years unfolding like those rotting leaves
I have forgotten many days from that time

I lean in toward the sound of the dinnertime cry
calling me from the emptied harvest fields
as I held the first reaping of self-love seedlings
little did I know what lay ahead for me.

I hasten to the precipice of the unknown
once I had a backpack filled with hope
ready to replenish me on those voyages
of mystery and imagination, mind whirring

I finally arrive at the calm devastation of the lake
I never thought I would depart from those days
there is something important to be said for
forgetting and re-membering these lessons

I am sprinting backwards
yet today
I have time.

studied.

dear seminary,

you have become a faithful friend
and a poetic provocation
prayerfully, I embark on
this intent investigation

each sacred second
every contagious crisis
lunchtime conversations and
the process of exegesis

there is something so beautiful
within all the classes and readings
about sneaking in poems and praises
between all the laughter and meetings
and questions.

oh, and the halls of your library
what wondrous places to unearth
doctrines of ages abounding
bound by a shared faith and work

thank you for aiding my journey
in unearthing my ageless appetite
hidden beneath those dim years
of my learning's lost delight

dear seminary,
you have helped set me free.

harvest fields.

when I was only a little one,

trained hands reached before me
searching, gathering sustenance
I observed, wide-eyed in wonder
the stalks far above my head

the wind and laughter guided me then
pushing me along the gold and green rows
I was safe and free, I cartwheeled along
my bare skin colliding into the soil

I am no longer that little one only.

I have learned, these days, the gathering
holds sweat before celebration
some toil, some twirling dance
and exertion alongside the breeze

there is hardly time to honor
the food I have fought to sustain
that keeps me going day by day
so that this spring I may plant a bit more

the little one and I walk hand in hand

respecting this serene, yet sturdy garden
that weathered storms I thought unsurvivable
and not only that, continued expanding
finding flower and fruit year after year

we have learned and loved this land well
and we receive its blessings with thanksgiving
there is much tilling, planting, and watering ahead
and yes, laughter and bright eyes and cartwheels

dear heart, you were made to bloom.

you.

your name is not simply beautiful
how base a term.

your inheritance
claims far more

you are a star-breather
a spirit conduit

you are moving poetry
and a wielder of divine weapons

you are a hope-seeker
a holy labyrinth

you are a sun refractor
and your crown is a song luminescent

yet more than all these
far greater, dear one

you are loved.

fed.

I wake
to a spiritual pantry
full of delicious bread and wine

there's been
so much growth in me
I find my soul finally prospering

I choose
now to walk
the garden path of devotion

taking
me towards
a promised land I know not

not yet, anyways.

(re)view.

watch the door.

dazzling darkness
compelling chaos

catch me.

I perceive eons past
my world kaleidoscoping

heart wide.

illuminated ignition
wistful whirlwind

wake up.

viewing your past anew,
will you now love it better?

watch the door.

"if given your life once more, how would you love yourself differently?"

(re)love is a poetry collection inspired by the daily struggles we face in our lives, including mental illness, self-love, inherited faith, and our shifting understanding of identity. Thematically situated around the earth and its greenery's life cycles, this collection explores concepts of spiritual growth, time, sexuality and gender, living with physical and mental health conditions, and the mystery that dwells within and among us. *(re)love* invites us to plant and cultivate new seeds of self-love and compassion, reminding us that *"relearning is welcomed by this tender earth."*

"These poems grip and liberate, they breathe you in and blow you suddenly elsewhere. With the liveliest insistence, with a succinct honesty so gentle that sorrows and hopes land like seeds in the soil of now, Michaela Atencio opens the reader into 'this gap/between time and eternity's collisions called the present.'"
—**CATHERINE KELLER,** Drew University

"*(re)love* is a tender journey into the honest and rich soils of self-reflection and compassion. Through the gifts of their own experiences, Michaela's poetry welcomes the reader to search our own depths and that of the world around us and find there a kind and loving divine embrace."
—**M JADE KAISER,** co-founder and director of enfleshed

michaela atencio is an MDiv student at Virginia Theological Seminary. They are a queer, neurodivergent theologian and artist living in Alexandria, Virginia, with their husband, Mitchell. In their free time, Michaela enjoys baking, thrift shopping, and creating art in various mediums.

www.wipfandstock.com

RESOURCE *Publications*
An imprint of *Wipf and Stock Publishers*

ISBN 978-1-6667-4884-0

9 781666 748840